RIVERS TO THE FEN
Rivers Cam, Great Ouse, Nene and other Waterways

VOL 8 English Estuaries Series

ROBERT SIMPER

Published by Creekside Publishing
ISBN 0 9538506 0 9

Printed by Lavenham Press
Lavenham, Suffolk

By the same author

Over Snape Bridge (1967)
Woodbridge & Beyond (1972)
East Coast Sail (1972)
Scottish Sail (1974)
North East Sail (1975)
British Sail (1977)
Victorian & Edwardian Yachting from Old Photographs (1978)
Gaff Sail (1979)
Traditions of East Anglia (1980)
Suffolk Show (1981)
Britain's Maritime Heritage (1982)
Sail on the Orwell (1982)
Beach Boats of Britain (1984)
Sail: The Surviving Tradition (1984)
East Anglian Coast and Waterways (1985)
Suffolk Sandlings (1986)
The River Deben (1992)
The River Orwell and the River Stour (1993)
Rivers Alde, Ore and Blyth (1994)
Woodbridge: A Pictorial History (1995)
Essex Rivers and Creeks (1995)
Norfolk Rivers and Harbours (1996)
Thames Tideway (1997)
River Medway and The Swale (1998)
In Search of Sail (1998)
Family Fields (1999)

CONTENTS

Cover; View of the Weir Pool at the head of the River Cam. (Author)

INTRODUCTION

The North Sea tides once flowed freely into the eastern side of England. Generations of unsung heroes have laboured away walling off this low land to confine the rivers into narrow banked channels. It is possible that the Romans started the process and the Anglo-Saxons carried on. The later medieval landowners, particularly monasteries, threw up earth banks to keep back the sea and cut neat channels to get the water away. They were not always successful, as there have been countless floods that have extended far inland. Over the centuries the tidal washes and fens became fertile farmland, but the main rivers became navigable. This is where our story begins, and the book attempts to unearth some of the maritime activities on the rivers and waterways after the reclamation of the Fens.

The main purpose of the many rivers and drainage channels in the Fens is to get the fresh water from the eastern Midlands and East Anglia down into the Wash as quickly as possible and to keep the low lying land free from flooding. Navigation of these waterways has always been a secondary consideration. In spite of this, the rivers and channels of the Fens and the adjoining countryside have a fascinating boating history, which has been largely overlooked. It is a story in two parts, the rise and decline of commercial trade and the gradual appearance of leisure craft.

Cambridge was the first place to have anything approaching leisure boating, but this fine University town does not appear to have considered itself part of the very down to earth world of the Fen drainage system. Cambridge, with its punts and eights, belongs to the same inland waterway world as Oxford and the Thames. It has even drawn on Venice for inspiration for its waterside architecture. Cambridge with its colleges by the lawn edged waterway and its bustling riverside public houses, is a very pleasant self-contained world. It is also a very public world; more people must visit the Backs at Cambridge than any other stretch of waterway in Britain.

I have tried to look behind the scenes at Cambridge and see what makes the river tick. To do this I received help, on punts, from Maurice Tyrell of the Two Tees Boatyard, Ron Engersent at Scudamore's and Paul Joyce at Trinity, while Rosalind Moad, Assistant Archivist at King's College Library, was also helpful in sorting out details about punting. On the rowing Cam, several college boatmen, particularly Tony Baker at Caius (Keys) and his son Brian Baker at Jesus, were particularly informative.

While writing *Norfolk Rivers and Harbours* I met Tony Sanderson and his son Steve, at Reedham, and they showed me their family photographs. In the Victorian period F. H. Sanderson of Cambridge was a photographer in partnership with Mr Clarke and he invented a plate camera. According to the Sanderson family legend, he 'sold plate camera rights for a lot of money'. He was also Commodore of the Cam Sailing Club in 1905. His son Herbert Sanderson started his career in photography, but did not like it, so he went into boat building. He had a yard beside the Cam at Water Street, Old Chesterton, where he hired out yachts, motor boats and dinghies during the summer and built and repaired boats in the winter. The Sanderson family was very keen on sailing, but remained keen photographers so that their trips down to the Fen Levels were often recorded with photographs and put into the family albums. In 1932 Herbert Sanderson and son Tony moved to the Norfolk Broads, where they felt there was more scope for the boat hiring business.

The Sanderson's photographs remained in boxes in a cupboard, where some got damaged by the damp, but after my first visit Tony Sanderson started identifying the photographs and writing details on the back. Sadly he died before completing the task. When I returned in 1999 Steve stopped work on rebuilding a wooden yacht and happily lent me the Cambridge photographs.

Help in identifying the Sanderson photos came from Rodney and Marion Bryant who had written a history of the Cam Sailing Club. Rodney kindly showed me the wonders of his editing package on his computer that could bring life back to old photographs. With these photograph books, however, I have tried to keep the accuracy of the old photographs, and resisted the temptation of re-creating images from former ages.

Mike C. Davies told me about the navigable head of the Great Ouse and the times when he won the junior section of the Bedford-St Neots canoe race in 1956-7 and later when he operated the Bryant boat building business. Ron Nightingale, who did a great deal of work with the Great Ouse Restoration Society generously supplied a full account of the exciting period which lead to the opening up of the river to Bedford. James Forsythe and Jayne Tracey kindly guided us around the Fens.

The Ouse winds its way through attractive farmland and former gravel pits and at Hartford Marina, General Manager Scott Deverell encouraged our research. Karen Murdock of the National Trust supplied information on their Houghton Mill, while at Hemingford Grey, just down stream Rodney Gidding was happy to tell me his family's history. At St Ives, Mick Jones was also keen on seeing the history of their river recorded, but it was really his father, Laurie Jones who was living in retirement in north Norfolk, who brought the old days on the river alive. He started a boat hire business at Huntingdon just after World War II and paddled in canoes up the deserted River Lark in an unsuccessful search for the old circle staunches from the eighteenth century commercial waterway. Laurie Jones, in his eighties when I met him, was still taking his boat out for a row every day. Love of the water is something you never loose.

The Ouse is almost three totally different rivers, from Bedford it winds through attractive farmland. Then it cuts through the wide, open skies of the Fens and becomes a brown tidal estuary at King's Lynn. Here one wild winter's night David Baddley and Tony Johnson showed me historic records of the Ouse Amateur Sailing Club, while a spring tide lapped at the walls of the clubhouse.

I greatly benefited from reading Dorothy Summer's *The Great Ouse, a History of a River Navigation* that was published in 1973, and John K. Wilson's excellent publication, *Fenland Barge Traffic*. Many thanks to all the helpful people at The Cambridge Collection.

My research into the River Nene started just after the effects of 1998 Easter Floods were still in everyone's mind. Heavy rain at Oundle on the River Nene in the Midlands caused the water to rise faster and higher than ever before and marine manager, Mark Nye, had hauled two dinghies into the chandlers and filled them up with goods from the lower shelves. Next morning both loaded dinghies were afloat and the whole marina, and Fairlines boat works were flooded. Mark had started work at Oundle in 1969 and this was the worst flood he had seen. Since he lived in the bungalow on site, he parked a tractor near the door ready for a quick get away through the water, but fortunately the water level had started to fall by the morning.

Just across the road at Barnwell Mill, an old water mill converted to a restaurant, the Nene rose to flood the ground floor bar to a depth of 5ft and the swans were swimming over the fence along beside the back channel. At St Neots Marina Richard Brearley explained that the floodwater had flowed into the buildings and destroyed a board with many of the early photographs of the development of the motor boat berths.

The Jackson family of Stanground were most helpful, particularly Sheila and Peter Conning. Sheila remembered being put on a horse aged three when Vic Jackson's barges were being towed up from the 'Dog in a Doublet' lock. Peter recalled building boats at Stanground and going off to do a small job, in about 1953, in the last of the old wooden lighters. H. J. K. Jenkins of the Fen Lighter Project was very helpful in providing information, to get the Fen Lighter drawings correct. Ken Lockwood kindly spent hours trying to get the detail as accurate as possible.

Thanks to David Green, the East Coast artist, who went to considerable trouble with the maps and to my wife Pearl, who helped correct the proofs, and also shared my enthusiasm for exploring the rivers and backwaters to discover the past of these fascinating waterways.

RS Ramsholt

The Fen waterways have their own terms.

Clunch.	Chalk
Drove.	Road, usually on top of a river wall.
Gault.	Clay
Halingway.	Horses walked on a towpath, to haul the barges.
Hythe.	The Old English word for a quay
Key.	A windlass.
Lode.	A man made tributary of the main river.
Pen.	A lock chamber.
Penstock.	Ground paddle.
Piece.	Open space.
Slacker.	Gate daddler
Sluice.	The Fen Rivers word for A pound lock.
Spreads.	Oars, on barges at Cambridge.
Sprit.	Steering pole on a Fen barge.
Staunch.	Originally a single gate lock.
Turf.	Peat used for household fuel.

Source of Photographs
Steve Sanderson 22, 23, 41, 45, 46, 47, 54, 56, 86, 87, 89, 90, 116. Norfolk Wherry Trust 38. Cam Sailing Club 42,43, 44, 48, 49, 50, 51, 52, 53, James Forsythe 59. David Green 2, 33. Mike C. Davies 66. Cambridge Collection 15, 18, 24, 108. Ron Nightingale 67, 68. St Neots Museum 69, 70, 72, 73, 74. Laurie Jones 60, 75, 77, 80,88, 92, 93, 95, 97, 98, 102, 106, 119. British Waterways 125. Bob More 84. Steve Lowing 83. K. C. Lockwood 105, 106. F. C. LeManquais/Thomas Middlemass 81,82. Alan Faulkner 109. Sheila Conning 107, 133 134,135,136,139,140,143. Wisbech Museum 144. Barry Pearce 137. Environment Agency 124. Nick Hardinge 138, 141, 142. Laurie Johnson 60, 114. K. H. Kent 118. Bob Partis 103, Oundle Marina 127, 128..

Frontispiece. A seemingly timeless scene with Tyrrell's and Scudamore's punt rafts at Magdalene Bridge in 1999.
  This appears to have been the first place that the River Cam could be forded easily and the Iron Age people started a settlement on the north bank. The Romans made this the crossing point of one of their roads and the Normans built a wooden castle to defend this crossing.
Later the Great (Magdalene) Bridge replaced the ford, and a causeway was made on either side. The medieval town of Cambridge grew up around the Great Bridge. From this street a number of narrow alleys lead down to hythes where commodities such as salt, sedge and wine, were brought in. The closing of Denver Sluice in 1651 prevented sea going ships from reaching Cambridge and the character of the riverside area changed.

Chapter One
CAMBRIDGE AND THE RIVER CAM

1. A canoe and punt on the River Granta in about 1922. It is the river Granta until it reaches the Mill Weir, when it becomes the Cam. The Mill Weir holds back the water to create a deeper river than the Cam.

2. Punts for hire near the 'Anchor' in 1939. In 1874 Mark Johnson was building boats at the Anchor boathouse beside the Weir Pool. After him came Thomas Robson who hired out boats, while his wife Sarah ran the 'Anchor'. The Granary beside the 'Anchor' was built in 1840, but between 1914-20 it was F. H. Dolby's Boat Building Works. He then sold it to F. Scudamore who had started hiring out boats and Thames punts from his stations at Weir Pool and Magdalene Bridge in 1906.

F. Scudamore died in 1939 and the business, which had seventy-one punts and forty-five canoes, was sold to George Reynolds. The Cam punt hire business was continued as Scudamore Boatyard Ltd. In 1999 they had some 160 punts and were by far the largest of the punt hirers. Stan Tyrrell, a former employee of Reynolds, started a punt hire business in 1954 and in 1998 Mrs Tyrrell had twenty-two punts.

3. Scudamore's punts at the Weir Pool in 1999. From here the Cam flows along the 'Backs' of colleges including Queen's, King's, Clare, Trinity Hall, Trinity and St John's. The beamy Chauffeur punts were first allowed on the Backs in 1975 and are often manned by undergraduates. The demand to go on the Backs has become so great that two 8-people punts are often chained together to make a super-punt. The hire punts are the last wooden working boats, being built regularly, in England.

4. A horse towing a gang of flat-bottomed Fen lighters past Clare College in about 1815. On the right the 'haling' horse is wading along the sunken causeway. The causeway was built because the colleges refused to have a towpath or 'haling way' in their grounds. There are different types of Fen barges, a round bowed barge is in front, flat bowed next and the living lighter is after that.

5. A barge discharging a cargo at Queen's, on the Cambridge Backs, in the early Victorian period. There were bitter conflicts of interests between the Fen bargemen and the University Colleges of Cambridge. The members of the University were greatly offended by the swearing of the bargemen, in their traditional blue waistcoats and fur hats, as they struggled to work their craft along the Backs. In order to try and improve the situation the Jesus lock was built in 1835, slightly up steam of the previous one. The idea was to make the water deeper so that the time the barges took to pass up the Backs was cut from half a day, to an hour. However the horses then had to struggle up the Backs in even deeper water.

6. A punt passing King's on the Backs at Cambridge in 1946. At Cambridge the punts are propelled by a person standing right at the stern, while on the Thames, the punter stands in the middle.

43817. CAMBRIDGE: CLARE BRIDGE & COLLEGE.

7. The Backs, at Cambridge, in about 1920 with Clare Bridge and College, and King's College Chapel. The first Clare Bridge was built in 1326 but the local architect Thomas Grumbold designed the present one in 1638. The man on the left is in a double-ended clinker Fen boat. Watermen propelled the Fen boats with quants resting on their armpits as they walked along the side of the boat. The Fen boat was used until the Thames punts were introduced to Cambridge.

The present course of the River Cam through the Backs is artificial, the natural river being slightly to the west. Bin Brook and the backwater opposite King's College appear to be the remains of the old channel, but the present channel was dug around the thirteenth century.

Cambridge, View on the Cam, Trinity College Bridge.

8. View of Trinity Bridge in about 1912. Two of the punts are being propelled by women and it is believed that the Cambridge practice of punting, while standing right in the stern of a punt, was adopted because women from the colleges found this easier.

On the right is Strange's Raft, where punts, skiffs and canoes were hired out. Trinity let this boathouse to Strange who hired out Oxford punts and rowing boats. Before 1914 he didn't have to pay rent, but he had to have all the boats lifted out of the water for Sundays.

4

9. The Trinity punt station just below Garrett Hostel Bridge in 1999. In about 1930 Trinity had started its own Punt Club based at the Boathouse which was formerly rented to John Strange. In 1973 Paul Joyce started to build punts for Trinity in their Boathouse. In 2000 the Trinity Punt Club owned around 20 punts, some of which are hired out in the summer time. The Trinity punts all have names with some connection to 'three' and are used on the river from April until October.

10. Paul Joyce, with Gavin Simpson, building their version of a single decked 21ft saloon Camford punt called *Hat Trick*, in the Trinity Boathouse in February 2000. Wooden hire punts should last over twenty years, but those used by undergraduates often only last about ten years.

The wooden piece on the punt's bow is called the huff, an old Thames word for bow, while the 'walls' (sides) are strengthened with three straight 'knees' to prevent the sides from splitting when punts collide or hit bridges.

66904 Cambridge, View on the Cam.

11. Punts outside Trinity in about 1930. At that time this would have been a crowded afternoon. In the Victorian times all Cambridge sewage went down the river until 1895 when the first sewage works were opened. After this, trips on the river rapidly became more popular. Punts were brought from the Thames to join the canoes and Fen boats, but in about 1897 two Pembroke undergraduates, had the first saloon punts built at Cambridge.

12. A barge in the early Victorian period being poled down river towards the New Bridge, better known as the Bridge of Sighs. This bridge links St John's with its accommodation in New Court. It was inspired by the Bridge of Sighs, at Venice, which prisoners had walked across on their way to their execution. The New Bridge at St John's was built in 1831.

After the Norman Conquest, Cambridge was developed as the port for the eastern corner of The Wash, but the centre of sea trade shifted down to King's Lynn later. The early medieval port of Cambridge is believed to have been on the east bank and had channels leading up to the warehouse behind King's Parade and Trinity Street. In 1996 the Cambridge Archaeological Unit located a medieval ditch in the grounds of St John's College. This was linked to the river and it was assumed that it led up to a hythe and warehouse.

13. A double decked Camford punt near the Bridge of Sighs in 1984. Originally square ended garden punts, and the double-ended Fen boats were used for pleasure trips at Cambridge, but in 1902 the 22ft Oxford punts were introduced. In 1964 R. F. Bell, manager at Scudamore's, decided that the Cam was too narrow for the Oxford punts and started to build smaller single decked 21ft Camford punts that could be turned around more easily. The early Camford punts had a deck at each end so that the punt person could go the opposite way by simply changing ends.

Cambridge. River Lane.

14. Looking down at F.W. Bullen's boat hire from Magdalene Bridge in 1905. The Fisher Lane houses were pulled down in 1932. Boat hire was already an active business in Cambridge in 1905, but at this time the Canadian canoes were very popular. It was through John MacGregor, who designed the 'Rob Roy' canoes and wrote a series of books about his adventures, that canoeing became popular. These canoes were flatter than the open Canadian craft.

Above: 15. Barges at the Hythe at Cambridge, in 1905, below Magdalene Bridge. This was the last commercial quay at Cambridge and had been the medieval Common Hythe. The colleges created lawns along the Backs so that by the Victorian period barge trade was confined to the Magdalene Bridge Quay side, above Silver Street Bridge, at King's Mill on the Cambridge bank and Bishop's Mill on the Mill Pool at Newnham.

The first people at Cambridge to have a steam tug towing barges were the Dants from the 'Cutter', Chesterton and their steam barge *Cutter* worked between Cambridge and Lynn. The steam barges that traded between Cambridge and King's Lynn usually towed up to three steel barges, known as 'scows'.

When Billy Collin had his timber yard taken over by Cambridge Corporation in 1909 he used the £3,000 compensation money to buy the 70ton *Nancy*, a steam barge which he ran until 1914. The barges *Enid, Lizzie* and *Eric* used to be loaded with ammonia at Cambridge Gas Works and then towed down to King's Lynn by the steam tugs *Olga* and *Nellie*. This trade finished in 1932 but during World War II Banhams tried to revive the trade with the Dutch barge *Nancy II*. She was too large for the Cam locks and also had difficulties with the tidal Ouse below.

Opposite top: 16 The crew of a punt *Mrs Simpson* stopped near Jesus Green Lock to buy a drink. King's punts are usually named after monarchs, but their punt *Mrs Simpson* is kept appropriately with *Edward VIII*.

On the left is the site of Strange's wooden two-storey boathouse. John and his son Don were boat builders and punt hirers here between 1865-1940. The Strange family claimed to have built the first punts at Cambridge, copies of the Thames punts that had been brought in. Their punts had raked knees like the Thames punts. Strange's hired out about fifty punts from their Chesterton Road boathouse and the rafts at Trinity.

In 1998 there were about 336 punts kept above the Jesus Green Lock. Sometimes at the height of the summer the river was so full of punts that it would have been possible to walk on them across the river without falling in. Punt hiring at Cambridge became big business so when a new firm, Blue River Punts started hiring them out at Mitcham's Corner, just above Jesus Green Lock, a period known on the river as the 'punt wars' began. The most public piece of the punt wars was in 1996 when punts were chained across the river to prevent Blue River from hiring out their punts.

Opposite: 17. This august gathering of Victorian gentleman are the Cam Conservators aboard their State Barge, just below the Jesus Lock in 1887. From here the Conservators voyaged down steam for their annual inspection which ended with a feast at their banqueting and meeting hall at Clayhithe. This State Barge, was built in 1851, was kept in a boathouse built specially for it, and was sometimes hired out on a daily basis.

The people of Cambridge were interested in developing the River Cam as a trade link with King's Lynn and were often at loggerheads with the Commissioners on the Middle Level as they put drainage first. The Cam Conservators were established by an Act of Parliament in 1702 for the sole purpose for improving the navigation of the River Cam from Byron's Pool, Grantchester, to Bottisham Lock, some thirteen miles down stream. This is a task they still perform.

18. Steam launch on the Cam at Cambridge in about 1907. The river below Jesus Lock has been used for pleasure for nearly a century. The College boat clubs had boathouses by the river and the town had the City of Cambridge Rowing Club, established in 1844 by the boat hirer James Fisher..

Opposite top: 19. The Cam seen from Victoria Bridge in 1906. The white barge appears to be an ex-ships lifeboat while the craft ahead, being punted, is the Cam Conservator's State Barge. Until 1952 H. C. Banham hired out punts below Jesus Green Lock, but these had high sides to cope with the wash from motor boats. Since then competitive rowing has taken over on this part of the river.

Opposite: 20.A marine ply cabin cruiser under construction at H. C. Banham's, Barge Dock, in 1966. In 1906 Charles Banham bought a small meadow beside the Cam, started a boatyard and adapted his craft for the new petrol engines. He had a fleet of self drive petrol powered launches and 45ft passenger boats operating a daily service from Cambridge to Clayhithe and weekly service to Ely. Before there were motor coaches Banham's launches were very popular. In 1920 Banham started a fleet of hire cruisers and in 1926 another fleet was started at Horning on the Norfolk Broads. After World War II the Barge Dock was often packed with Banham's craft. He had thirty-five hire cruisers, eight day-boats and three passenger-boats that ran to Ely. H. C. Banham died in 1953 and his business was eventually sold, in 1961, to Pye Ltd.

The Cam from Victoria Bridge, Cambridge

11

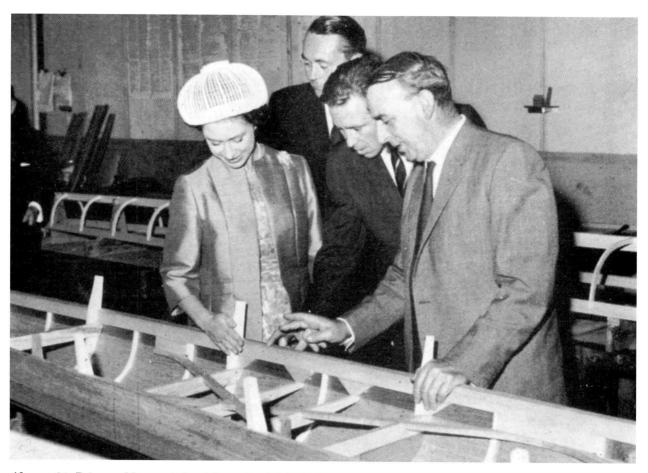

Above: 21. Princess Margaret, Lord Snowden, M. Bell of Pye Ltd. and J. A. Hodgkinson, in Banham's racing rowing boat department at Victoria Bridge in 1963. Herbert Charles Banham had bought Pocock's racing boat building business at Victoria Bridge in 1919. The yard had been started by Searle in about 1850 and was later owned by Pocock & Winter until the last of the Pococks emigrated to the United States to build racing boats there.

The Oxford and Cambridge University Boat Clubs had their eights built on the Thames, for the famous annual race there. However, in 1950 H. C. Banham built and eight for Cambridge, which won that year. After that Banham built the Cambridge boats. In 1965 Banham produced the first fibreglass single person, racing skiff. This was the most successful class of fibreglass racing boats in Britain.

Opposite: 22. The Cam Road Yard was the centre for Banham's hire fleet and boat building.

Opposite right: 23. The *Rogue,* one of Banham's fourteen motor cruisers he used to hire out from Cambridge. They also had four sailing yachts for hire.

Opposite below: 24. The Trinity boat and boathouse in 1870 with the boat building shed belonging to Logan on the left. This boat had won the Head of the River race, by beating the St John's boat and also won the Granta Challenge Cup by four lengths.

THE STARTING PLACE AT CAMBRIDGE

How to Get There :

From Cambridge Railway Station :

By No. 101 Bus Service to Haig Road and 5 minutes walk down this road.

Or by Taxi to bottom of Abbey Road.

Cars and Motor Cycles should come via Chesterton Road and Haig Road, (see map on back cover) driving straight through to Boatyard where they may be left at owner's risk for period of hire.

H. C. BANHAM, LTD.

Registered Office :

RIVERSIDE WORKS, CAM ROAD, CAMBRIDGE

Directors: H. C. BANHAM, C. L. BANHAM

M.C. 'ROGUE'

2 Length 28 ft., beam 6 ft. 10 in., draught 1 ft. 11 in. Very roomy single-cabin boat, having two spring berths, with sideboard and wardrobe. The long sliding sunshine roof gives plenty of ventilationt and head-room 5 ft. 2 in. under beams. Toilet right forward. Large galley including sink, draining board, and fresh-water tank under ; pantry and cupboards. Aft open cockpit is 9 ft. long, fitted with seats and lockers under. Waterproof awning. Engine is a 4-cylinder Brooke " Empire," self-starter, with reverse gear. Wheel steering with controls at hand. Electric light. All requisites for living and sleeping aboard are provided for two persons, except towels and linen. (Calor gas for cooking).

Terms per week : £9 10s. 0d.

25. The Lady Margaret's College boathouse, seen in about 1905. H. C. Banham, the Cambridge boat builder, purchased much of the bank of the Cam in 1908 and then re-let some of the riverside to the Colleges for boathouses.

26. Caius College's Boathouse in about 1905. The Caius College Boat Club was started in 1827. Their present Boathouse, built in 1881, is the oldest at Cambridge. In 2000 Caius had five eights for men and three for women.

27. Jesus College's Boathouse in about 1905. This actual boathouse was burnt down. Evidently hot asphalt put on the shower room floors, smoldered away and set fire to the building. These boathouses were often flooded until the river was dredged between 1922-33.

28. The Cambridge University Boat Club's Goldie Boathouse is a well-proportioned building built in 1911. J. H. D. Goldie of St John's and Steve Fairbairn played an important part in promoting rowing at Cambridge. In the 1870s John Goldie, son of the vicar of St Ives, was the stroke for the Cambridge boat, in the University Boat Race on the Thames against Oxford, and he took part in this race three times.

29. An Emmanuel eight in the Chesterton reach about 1933. The Horse Grind Ferry in the background was at the bottom of Ferry Lane to Stourbridge Common. A bridge was built and the Horse Grind and Pike & Eel ferries closed in 1935.

30. Ferry at the 'Pike & Eel' in about 1910. There were two ferries here, a large one for horses and carts and a punt for foot passengers. Both ferries were hauled across the river on chains. When coming up river, this was the first of five Cambridge ferries.

31. This shows the 'Pike & Eel', in about 1910. A stall in front of the pub appears to be set out to sell food to passing rowers.

32. Maurice Tyrell building a wooden 21ft Cambridge Punt at Two Tees Boatyard in 1998. The older wooden planked punts always had trouble with the bottoms leaking and the marine ply punts have lasted longer. Built of mahogany ply the Two Tees punts had 14 inch high sides, higher than most, and the deck on the stern was longer. Maurice built a punt 'on spec' every winter and they were then sold to the college punt clubs, notably Queen's, Magdalene, Jesus, St John's, Wolfson, and Darwin. As the TT and Tyrell punts have higher sides they can be sold to other rivers where there are problems with the wake of passing motor boats.

This boatyard was started in the late Victorian era by Ted Mathie and then sold to Lister in 1939. In 1968 Maurice Tyrell and Ernie Tile, who had been boat builders at Banham's, bought the yard and named it Two Tees, after their surnames. Actually Maurice said 'I never left Banham's, they left me'.

33. A bump being made in the May's Races of 1939. Because the Cam is a narrow river a Knock Out regatta, known as the Bumps, is held for College eights. Each Division of eighteen boats starts at Baits Bite Lock, with each boat 90ft apart, and the object is to touch or bump the boat in front. The two boats then pull to the side and allow the others to continue racing. The boat that bumps the one ahead is moved up a place in the next Division start. On the final day the overall winner becomes the Head of the River and returns to the Boathouse amid much celebration.

34. Eights racing in the final 'getting on race', Lent 1909.

35. The crowd gathered in 1911 at the Ditton Corner for the May Week Bumps Races. The Mays were started in 1827 because of the rowing rivalry between St John's and Trinity. In 1852 they were divided up into Divisions. The races were held in May but later on they were moved to a post-exam period, in June.

36. Ditton Corner in the wet 1998 Bumps races. The Cambridge University, Women's Bumps Races started in 1974 with fours and in 1990 eights were introduced. Each Division starts in the Ditch Reach goes around First Post Corner into the Gut, where most bumps take place, around Grassy Corner into Plough Reach and then around Ditton Corner to finish in Long Reach.

37. A 1998 Bumps race. The Clare boat is against the bank after a successful bump. In the background the Robinson boat is chasing the Jesus boat around Ditton Corner into the Long Reach and the finish of that Division. The Head of the River that year, and the following year, was Caius.

38. The Fen Lighter *Black Prince* shortly before she was taken to Cambridge Museum of Industrial Archaeology in 1974. Once out of the water the barge deteriorated rapidly. To save the hull from being burnt Eric St. John-Foti moved her to Downham Market.
This barge was one of many which were sunk in the Roswell Pits at Ely and fifty people spent three years building a dam around her and after several attempts finally succeeded in lifting her. The original Fen barge was a clinker built craft with a curved bow, but later ones were like the carvel built *Black Prince*. These barges were around 47ft long and loaded 20-25 tons.

39. Baitsbite Lock at Milton, Cambridge in about 1935. Below this there used to be a lock at Clayhithe, which was replaced by the Bottisham Lock.

40. Bridge Hotel, Clayhithe in about 1910. When Banham's tripper boat *Countess Bury* reached Clayhithe Bridge the wheel was quickly unbolted and taken off so that she could get underneath. The boat was left to steer herself until she came out the other side and the wheel was then quickly fastened on again.

All barges passing Clayhithe had to pay a toll to the Cam Conservators. When the horses were hauling the gangs of barges, it was not wise to stop them because it was heavy work getting the gangs going again. A man had to get off the leading barge in the 'cock boat', pay the toll, and get back on the last barge as it went past.

41. Members of the Cam Sailing Club and their boats being towed down the Cam in 1901. They were on their way to the first Summer Camp at Ely, an event that became a main feature of the club's program. They sailed to different places during a social week and their ladies joined them by train on Thursdays.

42. Mr Roper about to start a Cam SC Race at the Summer Camp in about 1935. The Summer Camps continued until 1938 but the year before this they went to the St Ives Regatta and had a very sociable time. It seems they had great difficulties getting there because the Great Ouse was so shallow.

43. The *Olga*, No 12, racing at Clayhithe in 1910.

44. Boats from the Cam Sailing Club seen at Waterbeach in 1920 for the unveiling of the club's War Memorial. When the Cam Sailing Club was founded in 1899 they held their first regatta in the Long Reach just below Cambridge, but they soon moved down to Waterbeach where they built their first clubhouse in 1905.

The yacht club was an important part of the Cambridge town scene and the member's ladies came down by car on Sundays dressed in hats, silks and fox furs. The ladies did not take part in the boat racing, but played croquet on the lawn. The Cam SC bought the surrounding meadows and this helped its growth into a family club.

45. The half rater *Volunteer* was originally raced at The Ouse Amateur Sailing Club at King's Lynn, but was later sold to a member of the Cam Sailing Club and raced regularly on the Cam. She was sailing until about 1974 and was still being stored ashore in 1999.

46. The Sanderson family, having a holiday on the houseboat *Miss Hook,* at Waterbeach in about 1915. This houseboat was poled along. Most of the Cam SC members were tradesmen and they used to cycle down the halingway to enjoy the racing on Thursday afternoons, early closing day in Cambridge.

47. The Cam Sailing Club's Regatta at Waterbeach in about 1925. The *White Heather* is in the foreground. Herbert Sanderson maintained Mr Pye's yacht and used to helm it during the races while the owner crewed. If they did not win, the owner is reputed to have used harsh words.

48. The Sanderson family cruising in the Fen Country, on the gaff sloop *Sprite,* in about 1930. Tony Sanderson is on the stern and Herbert Sanderson is on the right. They cruised out on the Wash in this sloop and she also used to be hired out.

Above: 49. The Cam Sailing Club's Clubhouse flooded in 1937 with the *Miss Hook* on the right. There is a hand-operated sluice in the foreground, which lead into the remains of Waterbeach Lode where barges had gone, before 1914, to load at the station. The Lode silted up and a new drain ditch was dug. In 1972 this was dug out and a launching slip was created for the Cam Sailing Club and the Cambridge Motor Boat Club.

The Cam Conservators tried to cut down the amount of flooding when they began weed cutting in 1938. There was bad flooding again in 1978 when two inches of rain fell on Cambridge in twenty-four hours. The problem was not really solved until about 1986 when the Cam was dredged deeper so that water could get away quicker.

Left: 50. This is one of the University Cruising Club's scows that raced at Waterbeach in the 1930s. These Cambridge scows were punts fitted with sails.

51. In about 1957 Cam SC member John Hookham tried to overcome the expense of having a wooden boat by building one of paper. Its mast was also built of newspaper stuck together with aerolite resin glue. The 'paper boat' *No Hurry* sailed successfully on the Cam for several years, and was the forerunner of mass-produced grp hulls, which made dinghy racing available to more people.

52. The steam tug *Nellie* towing the barges *Bertie* and *Gladys* near Bottisham Lock in 1927. The steam barges took twenty-four hours to reach Lynn from Cambridge, but a round trip took about a week.

53. The tug *Aledia* towing sugar beet barges on the Cam in 1927.

54.   The Sanderson family with their boat, rigged up for sleeping aboard, in Burwell Lode near Upware Lock in about 1910.

55. The narrow boat *Skylark,* just after passing through Upware Lock into Reach Lode in 1984. There had long been a few pleasure craft kept at Upware, but berths for motor cruisers were started in 1977.

56. The Sanderson family near the turf sheds at the head of Wicken Lode in about 1908. The turf load boat, astern of the Sanderson family's sailing boat, was used to take the turf down to Upware Lock where it was loaded on to barges that went to Cambridge or Lynn.

57. Harold Sennitt, of Wicken, seen at Upware in 1984. He told us that he was the last Fen turf digger and that he had worked beside Reach Lode. Once there had been around two hundred men hand cutting turf for household fires. Local housewives bought the turf in 'hands' of 60 or 'half hands' of 30. The local 'turf float' boats took the turf to Cambridge where it was sold in 'thousands', but there were actually only 600 turf in a 'thousand'. Harold Sennitt said he used to cut 'forty thousands' a year.

He remembered that when the water was high, the Upware Lock was left open and gangs of eight Fen barges were towed through, loaded with sugar beet, 'clunch' or fertilizer from The Prentice Manure Works, on Burwell Lode.

Opposite top: 58. Burwell Lode, seen in the 1930s. At the head of the Lode the 'Weirs' turned to the north while the 'Anchor Straits' turned south. In the past the Anchor Straits had been used by sea going ships, but in later years the lighters used the Weirs. The waterside properties in Burwell ran down to the Lode in narrow strips so that they all had their own hythe, and often a warehouse. In the 1870s there was a boom in digging coprolite for phosphate fertilizer along the Cam. Barge traffic increased as coprolite was taken from the Lodes and from Cambridge to King's Lynn. Then a fertilizer factory was started on Burwell Lode with its own barge yard. Prentice, and before that, Colchester & Ball, ran a barge yard at Burwell and the last barge built, in 1914, was the *Ready Money* for Archie Jackson of March. Barges were still repaired here until 1938.

Opposite right: 59. James and Mary Forsythe in their boat *Detritus* at the head of Reach Lode in 1976. At that time the Fen waterways were being opened up for pleasure cruising. Reach Lode may have been dug by the Romans to an inland port at the end of the Devil's Dyke. In the medieval period Reach had an annual fair, and sea going ships came up for it. In the 1930s Vic Jackson's gangs of lighters loaded the clunch away from Reach. They took three days to make the trip through Stanground sluice and on to Peterborough. The last trade from Reach and Burwell Lodes was sugar beet for Ely Factory.

MAP OF CAMBRIDGE

1. Coe Fen beside the River Granta.

2. Robinson Crusoe Island. In the Victorian period Thomas Robson and then F.H. Dolby of the 'Archor' had punts for hire at Robinson Crusoe Island. The site of Grantchester Mill which was destroyed by fire in 1928, marks the end of boat navigation and above this is Byron's Pool where the poet swam. There was a Roman wharf at Grantchester.

3. Sheep's Green grazed by cattle in the summer.

4. Newnham Mill Pool. 'Granta Inn'. There were two water mills at the head of the Cam and the millers are reputed to have been deadly rivals. It seems that the miller at Newnham was a rogue because he took his rival's water and then charged the bargemen, during a drought, for the release of 'flashes' of water. The Newnham mill was burnt down in about 1850 and the King's Mill pulled down in 1928. 'Garden House Hotel' on the site of the miller's house.

5. Charles Darwin owned the 19th century Newnham Grange. The house and former mill granary are now part of Darwin College.

6. Laundress Green.

7. Weir Pool with 'Anchor Hotel' and the Anchor Yard with Scudamore's Boatyard and office just above the weir.

8. The Mathematical Bridge at the top end of the Backs. This wooden bridge at Queen's College was built in 1749 to mathematical principles, without nails. The original bridge was replaced in 1843 and again in 1958 but bolts were used because the original method could not be emulated.

9. As the college officials would not allow horses to walk through their grounds the Cam Conservancy built a sunken causeway through the Backs. Horses pulling the barges waded on the causeway up to their bellies as they hauled the barges up to the Mill Pool. Parts of the paving remains, particularly near St John's, and punt poles often get stuck in the crevices between the stones causing the unfortunate punter to fall into the water.

Clare College Bridge built by Thomas Grumbold in 1638. The middle arch appears to sag, and there is a legend that a Clare College man stood on the bridge and made it sag under his weight, because he was so proud of receiving the mathematics tripos. At Cambridge the tripos is the final examination for the BA degree.

10. Scholar's Piece. The meadow opposite King's College Chapel has been kept open, in spite of plans to build on it, in order to provide a good view of the King's College Chapel. The head gardener makes arrangements with a local farmer to graze cattle on this land during the summer and autumn, to keep the grass short.

11. Trinity College Punt house. It appears that in the early medieval period the inland Port of Cambridge may have been in the area now occupied by the colleges. There were lanes leading down to corn, flax and salt hythes but when the colleges were built, barge traffic was forced above Silver Street Bridge and confined to the Quayside.

12. Robert Rumbold built Wren's Bridge or Kitchen Bridge in 1709-12 to Sir Christopher Wren's design. The second St John's bridge is the Bridge of Sighs or New Bridge built in 1831 and modelled on the Bridge of Sighs in Venice.

13. Bin Brook with St John's Punt Harbour at the mouth. St John's New Court, built in 1831 is just up river and lighters brought food and turf to the door which was level with the water.

14. The Great, or Magdalene Bridge. This bridge was built in 1835 on the site of the Roman crossing point over the River Cam and Cambridge grew up around this point.

15. Cambridge's medieval Common Hythe. In the Victorian period it was Bridge Street Wharf. In the 1930s when Cambridge had ceased to be an inland port the area became very run down, but was redeveloped as the Quayside for punt hire and a very pleasant tourist centre. Just down river a block of flats has replaced the electricity generating station.

16. The site of Strange's Boathouse, where boat building and punt hire took place until the boathouse was pulled down in about 1962.

17. Jesus Lock. The iron bridge was built over the river in 1892 to replace the wooden bridge.

18. College Boathouses.

19. Midsummer Common. The next open green is where Stourbridge Fair was held. This great medieval autumn trade fair was started, in 1211, by a charter from King John. The Fair, held on an open field worked by strip holders, could not start before the corn was harvested, and the stalls had to be off by Michaelmas Day so that the land could be ploughed. The fair was held here so that the Merchants could arrive in sea going ships.

20. The Dant family operated the Cutter ferry until it was taken over by the Cam Conservancy. Dant also owned the Barge Dock, now just up-river of Elizabeth Way. This had become one of Banham's three boat yards, but was redeveloped in 1998 as waterside flats with a boat harbour.

21. 'Fort St George in England' is named after Fort St George in India. The public house originally stood on an island in the Cam and there was a sluice here. The Cam Conservators also had their tolls collected here. In 1835, Jesus Lock was rebuilt, the sluice and weir were removed and river deepened and widened. The Pauley family ran a chain foot ferry here until 1927 when it was replaced by the suspension bridge.

Artemis Baitsbite Lock, 1987.

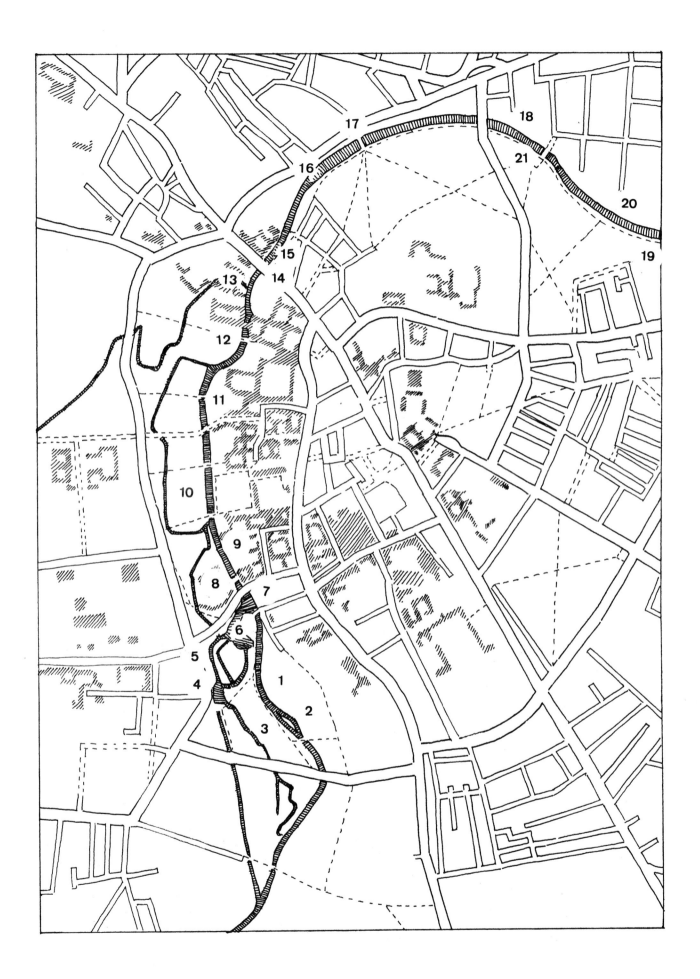

Chapter Two

RIVER GREAT OUSE, AND THE WEST NORFOLK RIVERS.

60. The Bedford Regatta, 1851. It is assumed that both the Anglo-Saxons and the Vikings used the waterways to reach the middle of England, but there is no real evidence for this. In the medieval period there was trade up all the rivers from the sea, but evidence is again patchy. However after 1600 the trade did increase the importance of the whole area. The river navigation was improved so that by 1630 barges were able to reach St Neots. It was not until 1689 that the Ouse was navigable right up to Bedford.

61. The Town Bridge over the Great Ouse, at Bedford in about 1906. This bridge was built in 1813 to replace the

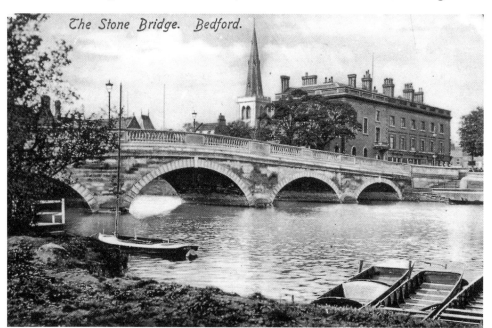

early narrow medieval bridge that used to hold up the flow of the water.

There are seventeen locks between Bedford and the Wash, some seventy-five miles. There was always trouble with silting in the navigation up to Bedford, particularly in the upper reaches, and regular barge traffic petered out in about 1870. In 1883 Leonard Simpson, a successful stockbroker, acquired the navigation rights and restored the locks up to St Neots in 1893 and up to Bedford in 1896.

62. Hire punts at Bedford in about 1910. The Embankment, across the river, had been the site of wharves, became private and in the 1880s became public gardens. There were more wharves on the north bank. Many of the properties in St Mary Street had curved boundary lines to make room for a shop, with a wharf by the river, where coal, timber and other goods were brought in.

63. This picture shows a tripper steamer at Bedford, in about 1910. Leonard Simpson's attempt to re-introduce river trade was very popular at Bedford, but was thwarted by Huntington County Council. They started a legal battle to have the right to open the sluices during times of flooding and to navigate the river without paying tolls. Simpson gave up the struggle and in 1906 rented out the locks, at Bedford and Great Barford, to the Ouse Locks Committee so that pleasure craft could use the upper reaches. That summer 1,800 boats passed through Bedford Lock, but the navigation was closed by weed below Cardington.

64. Hire skiffs at Bedford in about 1925. In the background is the bowstring Suspension Bridge, which was built in 1888 at a time when the banks of the Great Ouse River were being landscaped.

65. Bedford in 1925, at the top end of Duck Mill meadow island. In 1920 C. F. Farrar reported that all the Great Ouse locks above St Ives were unworkable, although people were still making trips along the Ouse in canoes. In 1930 the Great Ouse Catchment Board bought Simpson's rights of navigation and restored the locks from Brownshill right up river to Tempsford. World War II stopped further work. A rally of boats was held at Kempston in 1949 and in 1951 a meeting in Bedford Town Hall, which was attended by Peter Scott, led to the forming of the Great Ouse Restoration Society. This Society then campaigned and raised funds to restore the five derelict upper Ouse locks so that craft could navigate up to Bedford.

66. The start of the Bedford-St Neots canoe race in about 1953. The Picturedrome Cinema was demolished about ten years later to make way for the County Hotel. Chetham the boat builders and hirers, seen on the left, have been replaced by Bedford Rowing Club. Ernie Bryant was also a boat builder and hirer on the Embankment, but Bedford Council moved him to a site near the Rowing Club. Mike C. Davies bought Bryants in 1965 and tried to revive punt hire, using grp punts. As well as hiring, Mike Davies built about fifty 10ft and 14ft grp rowing and sailing boats, but gave up the business in about 1975. Mr Smith used to run pleasure trips down river, from the steps near the bridge, with a 50ft electric launch.

67. The Duke of Bedford, seen aboard *Filomela* in 1972, when he officially opened the new Roxton Lock and Weir. The Great Ouse River Board restored the Bedford Lock in 1956, but the guillotine lock was deliberately kept low to discourage motor cruisers from going to the upper level, an area kept for rowing.

68. Ron Nightingale's *Filomela* leaving the new Great Barford Lock in the procession up to The Castle Mill Lock in 1978. The new lock and weir let considerably more water through than the old staunch. After the opening of Castle Mill lock boats could travel from Bedford right down to the open Wash again.

The Cardington Lock was reopened in 1963 as part of a land drainage scheme, but the Great Ouse Restoration Society paid for the pointed lock doors. Because the derelict Willington and Barford Old Mill locks were quite close together only one new lock was built, at Willington. The site of the Barford Mill lock

was dredged through and the earth used to raise farmland on the south, and on the island. A new lock and weir were constructed further down river. The floods during the winter of 1974-5 slowed the Anglian Water Authority's work on the Great Ouse River when they were building a new lock and weir at Great Barford, but it was completed in 1976. At the same time the two old Willington weirs were replaced with a much larger one so that the grazing land above it was not flooded so much in the winter. To maintain the public footpath at Barford Old Mill, a new 20m footbridge was constructed.

69. The Five Arches dam at Eaton Socon in about 1910. The Mill at Eaton Socon was built in 1847 and closed in about 1962. In 1977 John Simmonds, Derek Young and Peter Ellis bought the mill as a centre for River Mill Boats hire fleet. River Mill Boats had 12 hire boats on the Ouse and four in France until 1987. After this the millstream and pond, which was dredged, became the Mill Boats Marina run by Duncan Simmonds.

70. The centre of the photograph shows the site of St Neots Marina. On the left is Gill's Boathouse Corner, St Neots at the mouth of the Hen Brook. In 1887 Charles Gill had premises, on the left, at 11 South Street, St Neots, and he had the wooden bridge over the Hen Brook built so that people could get down to his hire boat base at Boathouse Corner. Although Gill was not trained as a boat builder, he built over fifty Thames skiffs and punts. He converted an Ouse barge into the house-boat *Iris*, and built other houseboats that he let out to holiday-makers who came by train from London.

In 1922 the business was sold to Adcock, a sea captain, and in 1947 he retired and sold it to Alan and Jean Brearley. In about 1966 they gave up hiring out skiffs and motor boats on a daily basis and had the St Neots Marina dug. At that time plastic hulled motor cruisers were being mass-produced and this started the sudden growth of boating on the Ouse.

71. Looking up the Ouse from St Neots Bridge in about 1920. Gill's Boathouse Corner was the site of the present St Neots Marina. The boathouse in the back of the 'Old Falcon', on the left, originally had gates. This side of the river, at the back of the 'Old Falcon', seems to have been the site of the town quay from the medieval period until this area was built up in about 1848. The last barge traffic to St Neots brought imported timber up the Hen Brook, to builders C. G. Tebbutt's Navigation Wharf until about 1930.

The first St Neots Bridge appears to have been built in 1580 and this has been widened over the centuries. Through increased traffic in the late 1950s it was declared unsafe and the new bridge was opened in 1964. St Neots High Street was flooded during the 1947 Floods and again during the Easter Floods in 1998.

72. The hire skiffs and punts at the Bridge Hotel, St Neots, formerly the Half Moon, in about 1920. In the background is the Priory Brewery which was later the Jordan and Addington Mill. It became the Priory Centre in the 1970s and the St Neots Rowing Club is based here.

73. Rowing skiff on Weston Brook in about 1900. A similar skiff, built by Charles Waits of Cambridge, is in the St Neots Museum and is probably the oldest surviving boat from rivers leading to the Fens. Laurie and Harry Evans won 130 rowing trophies, on the Ouse, with this skiff between 1920-38.

The first rowing club was started at St Neots in 1860 and the main regatta races were against Huntingdon Rowing Club, with four oar boats. In the 1879 race the oars touched and although the St Neots boat finished first the Huntingdon umpire awarded the race to Huntingdon. This caused a major row and there were no further races for four years. In 1908 the Regatta and River Fete was started, and the Rowing Club was revived in 1912. Apart from in the war years, racing as gone on since then.

74. The Ouse Transport tug in the procession of decorated boats, which sailed from St Neots down to Little Paxton, in 1896, for the opening of St Neots Spa. In the late Victorian period St Neots was seeking to develop as a holiday centre for people from London. The opening of the Spa to sell Neotia Water, was a short-lived attempt to increase tourism.

75. Laurie Jones' steel hulled hire cruiser *Goosander* at the Paper Mill lock below St Neots in about 1958. Laurie Jones had four cruisers for hire at his yard at Huntingdon and later, until about 1975, from the St Ives Boat Haven.

The Great Ouse, Offord Cluny

76. Offord Cluny, 1964. When Brian Carter started the boatyard at Offord Cluny in 1949, the number of motor cruisers on the Great Ouse could have been 'counted on one hand'. Every so often he would take an open boat up to Bedford to maintain a right of navigation. He carried the boat around ruined locks on the way there and on the way back he went shooting through them.

Ballast was dug out on the Buckden side of the Ouse to construct the Grafham Water reservoir and Brian Carter turned one of these pits into Buckden Marina. He sold this in about 1979, and Carter's Boatyard in about 1987.

77. Laurie Jones' hire cruiser *Snowgoose* at Godmanchester in about 1958, near the Chinese footbridge that was built in 1827. Most of the boatyards and marinas on the Great Ouse started off with some hire cruisers, but later some gave up providing charter boats.

3436 THE OUSE AT GODMANCHESTER.

78. A foot bridge on the Ouse back channel at Godmanchester with the watermill in the background. The Godmanchester lock was restored in 1932 by the Ouse Catchment Board and fitted with one of the new guillotine doors at the head, but the lower pointed doors were retained.

THE BRIDGE, HUNTINGDON.

2368.

79. Huntingdon Bridge, in about 1904. In 1214 when this bridge was built, there was a regular river trade up to Huntingdon.

The Mills Godmanchester

80. Looking across the Ouse to Godmanchester from Huntingdon in about 1904. The Simpson's Ouse Transport Co. tug and barges are on the right. Behind these, with open doors, is the Huntingdon Boat Club, and boats are pulled up in front of Childs' boat hire shed.
    The Huntingdon Regatta took place in this reach. The shops in the town had half day closing so that the people could watch the regatta. Rowing races at Huntingdon were first organized in 1854 and by the turn of the century there were two boat-club houses on the east bank, just above the bridge.

81. Childs & Hall's boatyard at Godmanchester in 1948 with the white motor cruiser *Corsair* near the pontoon. In the background is the railway-bridge for the Kettering to Huntingdon line, a line that closed in 1959, and the A604 road-bridge was built in 1975.

This boatyard became Huntingdon Marine & Leisure owned by the Tyrrells, the Cambridge punt hire firm. They use it for storing punts and building new ones. In the 1940s the river used to turn violet when the cotton mill had a clean out and green when the pea factory released its waste.

82. The *Corsair*, a wooden motor cruiser berthed at Childs & Hall, near the bridge at Huntingdon in 1948. Godmanchester is on an important Roman crossroads where the Via Devana, from Colchester to Chester, crossed Ermine Street, that linked London and York. The medieval fourteenth century stone bridge in the background links Huntingdon and Godmanchester.

83. One of the Tyrrell's new Cambridge punts built by Steve Lowings at Marine & Leisure, Huntingdon, 1997. The punts are built and stored here and then go to Cambridge for hiring out in the summer.

84. This is a scene on the Great Ouse, in about 1912. On the left is the Hartford chain ferry that was used by farmers to take cattle across to graze on Westside Common. This ferry ran from a slopping hard in front of the pub and was still in use until about 1949. There was another smaller chain ferry about quarter of a mile up river that was used by anglers.

85. Rowing skiff from Huntingdon going down the Great Ouse in about 1912. On the right, the angler is sitting on the bridge that crossed Cook's Backwater. The trees on the left are just up river of the present Hartford Marina that was originally one of St Ives Sand and Ballast's gravel pits. Two local men bought the pits in 1967 and developed Hartford Marina. By 2000, there were 175 boats kept here. Just down stream is Daylock Marine, originally a RAF sailing club, which became a day hire boat centre in 1980.

86. Houghton Mill in about 1912. This large water-mill continued grinding flour until 1929. The tiny miller's office on the down river end was pulled down in about 1922.

87. The first record of a watermill at Houghton was in 969 when it was given to the Abbey of Ramsey. The present five storey mill was built in the seventeenth century and had one wheel which drove three grinding pairs of stones and two wheels on the southern side which powered seven pairs of stones between them. After Houghton Mill closed some local people wanted to pull it down, but it became a youth hostel. In 1939 Lt. Col. Louis Tebbutt gave it to the National Trust.

88. The newly repaired lock at Houghton in about 1895. This was part of Leonard Simpson's attempt to open up the Great Ouse again for commercial traffic.

89. The Sanderson family on a houseboat during their summer holiday about 1912. The houseboat is inside of the island at Hemingford Grey. There was another houseboat on the main channel.

90. Hire boats at Hemingford Grey in about 1912. Hemingford village regatta was started in 1904. There was punt racing, but the 'Vicar's Sculls' became the most famous of this unique event.

91. On the right is Gidding's boathouse at Hemingford Grey in about 1950. In the mid-nineteenth century John Gidding was building and repairing barges here, but in about 1885 his son John opened a business hiring out canoes and dinghies in the summer. John's son Jack continued the hire business, while his wife supplied teas in the upper storey of the boathouse.

Jack's son Rodney continued hiring, but the increasing number of motor cruisers was a problem. In 1969 three elderly ladies were out in Gidding's big punt when a passing cruiser swamped the punt with its wash and soaked the ladies. After this Rodney gave up the summer hiring. He had the boathouse pulled down and converted the two cottages into one. Just up river, at Hemingford Abbots, Hutson continued hiring out punts until the following year.

92. Hemingford Lock and Mill, seen from the upper level, in about 1895. During the 1894 floods Godmanchester Corporation opened the sluices at Godmanchester, Houghton and Hemingford. Leonard Simpson, who owned the Ouse Navigation, said they had no right to touch the sluices and brought a legal action against Godmanchester, but he lost the action.

93. In about 1895 the Great Ouse water level at St Ives was allowed to drop so that the sluice and bridge could be repaired.

94. The fifteenth century Tower Bridge at St Ives in about 1900. The chapel to 'St Leger', on the bridge, was built by the Abbots of Ramsey Abbey so that travellers could 'give thanks' for a safe journey, in the form of cash, to a monk who was stationed at the bridge. The Chapel became a small house and then a pub, but the top was removed early in the twentieth century.

   Fen barges were still discharging at the Town Quay, and there was a slipway, for repairing barges, further along Wellington Street. Above the bridge, barges used to go into an under-cover dock in the old Brewery. Barns had a boatyard just above this, which later became a site of The University Sailing Club.

95. The Town Bridge at St Ives in about 1950.

96. St Ives Town Quay, seen in 1999.

97. St Ives Staunch seen from the lower level about 1897.

51

98. This was a gravel pit that Laurie Jones bought in 1958 and developed into the Boathaven. When Laurie Jones came out of the RAF he rented a barn at Huntingdon, started a boat hire business and went on to build punts and sailing dinghies. Mr Banham of Cambridge told him "you will never make any money building dinghies; build motor cruisers for businessmen with secretaries and wives who are not very understanding!" Laurie Jones then built motor cruisers but eventually sold this business, and it became Purvis Boat Hire. In 1958 he purchased a gravel pit below St Ives. This had been dug by St Ives Sand and Gravel during World War II, to provide material for the construction of the Airfields. The pit had been purchased for £120, after the war, for angling and was later sold to Laurie for £700. Most people considered the pit to be a white elephant, but planning permission was granted to dig a channel to connect it with the Ouse and also to move a footpath. St Ives Sand and Gravel had been unable to get permission to move the footpath, but once it was re-routed, a channel was dug to link up all the pits, and the spoil was used to build the ground up higher than the 1947 flood level. When the St Ives Boathaven was opened in 1959 it was the first marina in Britain.

99. The motor cruiser *Sanguilla,* in 1999, bound up the Old West River. This was the old course of the Great Ouse after Earith. In the background is the 'Fish & Duck' at Pope's Corner were the Great Ouse and Cam join to form the Ely Ouse.

100. Clark and Butcher's roller mill at the head of Soham Lode in about 1906. Flour was sent by barge from this mill to Ely Dock and Chatteris, for shipment to London.

101. This shows Ely, in about 1910. Annesdale wharf, on the right is where cattle food was loaded. The 'Cutter' Inn, on the right was built in 1828 for the men known as 'cutters' when they dug the new Ouse channel between Adelaide and Littleport. On the left, Appleyard's Boathouse can be seen and the entrance to the Eastern, or Coal Yard Dock, which later became Annesdale Marine boatyard.

The main Ely Dock, which held up to three hundred barges, was to the south of the town, on Cawdle Fen. This

western dock was built after 1845-47 when Ely became a main railway junction. Coal came to Ely by railway and was shipped by water to many villages and farms that were only connected to the outside world by long muddy drove-ways. Most of this dock was filled in about 1914 and more in the 1940s, however some survived until 1963.

102. The 'Cutter Inn', at Ely, in about 1950. Until about 1935 timber was brought up by barge to the wharf just down river of the 'Cutter'.

103. Bill and Kathleen Leach on their steam launch *Artemis*, with 'Miss Harp', at the National Inland Waterways rally, Ely in about 1973. A. F. Leach (1901-89) was called 'Steamboat Bill' because he kept steam craft on the River Cam for over sixty years. The *Artemis* and Bill's previous steamer, the *Kathleen,* were kept at the Two Tees boatyard, Chesterton. He had bought the 21ft launch *Artemis* in 1951 just as she was about to be fitted with a diesel engine. The *Artemis* was built in 1899 by Summers & Payne, Southampton as a tender to the yacht *Artemis,* which in 2000 was under restoration at Hamburg. The launch *Artemis* originally had a quadruple-expansion engine and water-tube boiler by Simpson-Strickland of Dartmouth, but Bill installed a Merryweather vertical boiler that gave a speed of about 8 mph.

Below: 104. Sixty-nine year old Sid Merry watching his steel cruiser, *Lady Merry,* being re-launched at Ely Marina in March 2000. This cruiser was built in 1980, at Littleport, for boat charters. Sid Merry, the last eel catcher left on the Ouse, was born in one of the five cottages that stood on the present entrance to the Marina. These cottages were pulled down when the river was widened. The footbridge was built in 1964 and they started digging the Marina in 1980.

FENLAND LIGHTER GANG   c. mid 19th cent.

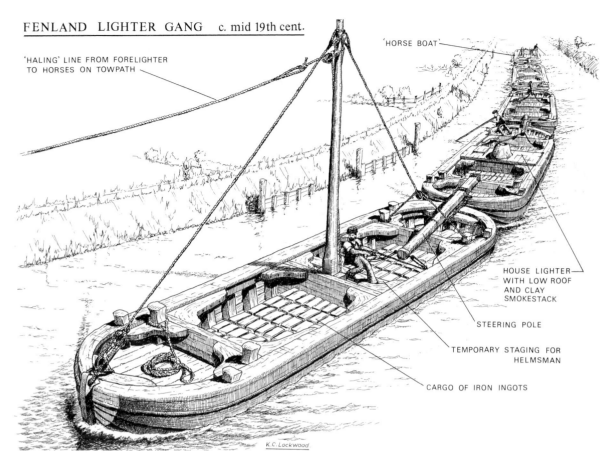

'HALING' LINE FROM FORELIGHTER
TO HORSES ON TOWPATH

'HORSE BOAT'

HOUSE LIGHTER
WITH LOW ROOF
AND CLAY
SMOKESTACK

STEERING POLE

TEMPORARY STAGING FOR
HELMSMAN

CARGO OF IRON INGOTS

K.C. Lockwood.

105. Ken Lockwood's excellent drawing of a typical gang of horse-drawn Fen Lighters of the 1860s.   When Denver Sluice was constructed in about 1651, it effectively closed the Ouse waterways to sea going craft. After this flat bottom inland Fen barges appeared on the waterways. These evolved out of the double-ended clinker craft, which had been used in the area since the Anglo-Saxon period. The Fen barges, or lighters, simply appear to have been larger versions of the Fen boats and smaller Turf boats. The lighters took over much of the work on the Ouse and Nene while the Fen boats continued to be used on the small rivers. In the eighteenth century the Fen barges loaded around 15 tons, but by the nineteenth century there were 20ton barges. Some of the 42ft fore-lighters loaded 30 tons. These barges were worked in strings or 'gangs', towed one behind the other, and had an ingenious steering arrangement of a 'sprit'.   In this way two men and a horse could move a long gang of six or more barges. A single square sail had been fitted to the larger fore-lighters, by 1700, so that they could sail with a fair wind. When the wind was against them the horse was put back on the halingway to tow the gang. At the aft end of the gang was the smaller Horse Boat, where the horses were kept. Some gangs had Houseboats for the men to live in.

FENLAND LIGHTER GANG   c. mid 19th cent.

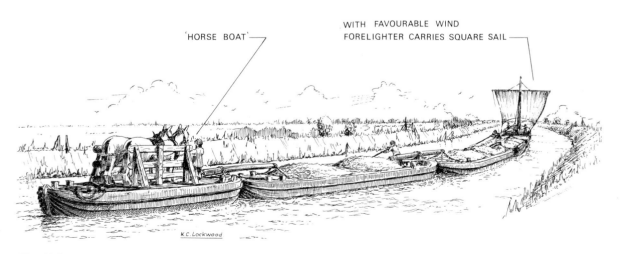

'HORSE BOAT'

WITH FAVOURABLE WIND
FORELIGHTER CARRIES SQUARE SAIL

K.C. Lockwood.

106. Fen lighter gang.

107. Fen barges going under the bridge at Littleport. The bargemen had just punted the gang under the bridge. The mast is mounted forward, which means that a horse is being used for towing rather than a steam tug. Frank Carr, in his book *Sailing Barges*, recorded that the last barge to use a sail was the *Pride of the Lark,* until about 1910.

108. The last commercial cargo carrier on the Fen River system was the 48ft tanker *Shellfen* that took fuel around to the pumping stations until 1975. The *Shellfen* was built in Holland in about 1912 and was brought to the Fens to carry bulbs, grown at Reach, to the railway dock at Ely. Shell converted her to a tanker to load 4,000 gallons, to replace the coal lighters that had been towed around to the pumping stations. Originally *Shellfen* supplied about hundred pumping stations, but the number dropped steadily as they were converted to electricity.

109. The gangs of steel dumb barges lying in the Ely Ouse at the Queen Adelaide sugar beet factory, Ely at Christmas 1926. During the winter months of the sugar beet campaign the tugs left Ely Factory, every morning, towing up to fourteen barges. Empty barges were dropped off at the farms and loaded barges towed back to the factory.

   The Queen Adelaide and Wissington sugar beet factories were opened in 1925 and King's Lynn in 1927. In the summer months 20,000 tons of coal were shipped up to them in barges from the Bentinck Dock, King's Lynn. The factories all relied on beet being brought in from the farms by water. The Water Transport Section, Ely alone had 150 craft, many of them purpose built rectangular steel barges that loaded 20 tons, but later on loaded up to 40 tons. Water transport stopped at the end of the 1958 sugar beet campaign, and the barges and tugs were sold. The Queen Adelaide Factory closed in 1980. Other barges on the Ouse brought timber from Lynn up to Jewson's at Earith until about 1937.

110. Abandoned Fen barges at the Two Locks Mildenhall on the River Lark in about 1913. In 1898, 7295 tons of coal came up to Mildenhall by barge, but the Navigation Company was wound up in 1900. On the Ouse and its tributaries, the horse that pulled the barge was trained to jump over the low fence as it walked along the haling way. The man did not get off the barge because the horse knew how long to wait to have enough slack rope to jump over the fence.

113. The 'Ship Inn' from where Brandon Creek, or the Little Ouse, runs up to Brandon, in about 1910. The lower reach of Brandon Creek is man-made, possibly Roman. Most of the rivers leading down to the Fen country were used for transport in the medieval period, although not much is known about the river trade until the canal age in the eighteenth century. Brandon Creek was navigable for the twenty-two miles to Thetford in 1664 and there was a long struggle to improve the river by fitting staunches. The peak was reached in 1845 when 15,000 tons of coal went up to Thetford, but by the 1890s the navigation was in poor repair. Some barge traffic continued up to Fison's chemical factory just below Thetford until about 1933 and after this only sugar beet barges came up to Wilton Bridge.

Opposite top: 111. A small 'turf float' barge hauled out for repair at the Gaspool, Barton Mills in about 1904. There was no more barge traffic up the Lark to Bury St Edmunds after 1894, but there was some traffic to Icklingham until about 1920. The navigation was sold to Parker Brothers, the Mildenhall millers, and they attempted to revive river traffic. In the 1920s some gravel was being taken by barge from Isleham and after this only sugar beet was loaded for the Ely factory. Barges sometimes went above the lock, but the tug waited at the lock and the barges had to be hauled back below the lock by the men.

Opposite left: 112. A gang of lighters with a steam tug at St Saviour's Wharf, Bury St Edmunds, in 1892 during a short-lived attempt to revive the Lark Navigation. The River Lark had been made navigable up to Bury St Edmunds in about 1720 and by the beginning of the nineteenth century 13,000 tons of coal a year reached Bury St Edmunds in horse drawn barges. Because of the staunches, a local form of lock, the journey up the Lark was very slow. After the railway reached Bury in 1848 the 23 mile Lark Navigation went into decline. The water in the Lark is very cold because it comes out of chalky ground.

114. The 'Ship Inn' showing the Great Ouse and Little Ouse in about 1938. In January 1928 the Great Ouse rose so that the floodwater was nearly level with the top of the river wall in front of the 'Ship'.

115. The four-arch bridge at Brandon, seen here in about 1920, links Norfolk and Suffolk.

116. Open Race, at the Denver Regatta in 1908. The first time that the Ouse Amateur Sailing Club, founded in 1881, and the Cam Sailing Club, met at Denver for a Regatta was in 1901. This is believed to have been the first inter-club racing in Britain. Members of the Ouse Open Boat Club often paid fishermen to race with them but the Club's name was changed to The Ouse Amateur Sailing Club when it was ruled that only owners could helm their boats during races.

117. Prize giving of the Ouse Amateur Sailing Club in 2000. The oldest cup here dates back to 1867 when the King's Lynn Royal Regatta was started for rowing eights. This faded out, and in 1881 a sailing regatta was started. Members used to keep their boats moored in the Ouse in front of the clubhouse. In 1960 the club moved most of their races to the Relief Channel at Southerly. The clubhouse in Lynn was flooded by high tides in 1953 and 1978.

118. The Lee family's barges at Alexandra Dock, King's Lynn, in about 1908. Robert Lee, right, started work as a boy on the barges in 1872 working from Sutton Bridge up to Northampton. This was before the Nene was improved up to Wisbech. Because of the disputes with landowners the halingway changed from one bank to another, particularly on the smaller rivers, and the horse had to be swum across with a man on its back. Sometimes this was done up to five times in half a mile, making progress very slow.

Hauling the barges was very hard for the horses because they had to go very fast to give the barges steerage-way. A gang towed by horse, with the tide, used to cover the fourteen miles from Lynn to Denver Sluice in about four hours. The demand for coal was at its peak in the winter, but the barges were often frozen up for long periods

119. This shows King's Lynn quay, in about 1910. Most of the small cargo ketches are billyboys from the Humber, while over on the West Lynn shore the yacht moorings can just be seen. King's Lynn grew up as the centre of river trade. Sea going ships brought in goods that were then taken up the Ouse and Nene to the Midland towns.

120. The Granary, King's Lynn, on Customs House Creek, with the sailing barge *Will Everard,* being loaded with wheat for Hull in 1955. To keep the berth open, men from the Granary had to shovel the silt into the creek channel and on the Sunday morning members of the fire brigade washed it away. Before 1939 the *Will Everard* had brought sugar beet from the Isle of Wight to King's Lynn factory and taken raw sugar away to Tate & Lyle's refinery in London.

Below: 121. This shows the Customs House Creek, King's Lynn in 1996. The Granary had been pulled down and Purfleet had been dammed up which resulted in the creek silting up quite quickly. In 1999 a dam was placed across the creek mouth and it was dredged out.

RIVERS TO THE WASH

1. Priory Marina. Bedford Corporation gave some of the cash they received for the abstraction of sand and gravel to become the decisive funding for the Ouse Restoration Project which resulted in the river being opened for navigation again in 1978. The ballast pits dug became the Marina and Country Park.

2. Leonard Simpson, who purchased the abandoned Ouse Navigation in 1883, had a house on the island below Great Barford. Simpson introduced steam towage on the Ouse and fought hard to regenerate the Navigation, but the local Councils put every possible obstacle in his way. They believed that if the locks were repaired, the flow of water would be stopped and cause flooding.

3. The River Ivel was turned into the navigation after the Act of 1757. Coal from Newcastle went up this river to Biggleswade and the navigation was extended to Shefford in 1823. Trade up the Ivel finished in 1876.

4. Tony Palmer moved from the Thames to start the Kelpie boatyard for pleasure craft at the old Great North Road Bridge, Tempsford in 1953 but in 1972 moved to Isleham Fen to start Fenland Boats.

5. Around 1900 there were two Bathing Places in the river at St Neots, one at the north of the town and the second at the Islands Common.

6. In 1930 the Drainage Board installed a sluice at the Houghton Mill to control the flow, but in the bad flooding in 1947 the Ouse flooded right up to the 'Three Horse Shoes' in the village square.

7. Hemingford water mill was pulled down about 1960. Later replaced by a sluice.

8. In 1947 there was a pub at Brownshill Lock, kept by the lock keeper which, because it was out of the sight of the eyes of the law, stayed open longer than licensing hours. This made it popular with boating people.

9. At Horningsea below St Peter's Church the Dock Lane still leads down to the water's edge where barges were once discharged. Coprolite was shipped out during the boom of the 1870s. Up stream a hundred yards, there was a cut off the Cam known as the 'Bricker' that was used by the local brick works, until about 1914, to bring coal in and take bricks out. Horningsea was the most southerly point that barges collected sugar beet from, for the factory at Ely.

10. Bottisham Lode was mainly used for moving farm produce in small boats.

11. Commercial End with its Merchants House and warehouse of 1662 was the wharf for Swaffham Bulbeck. In 1790s corn was being shipped to Newcastle and coal came back, and wine was shipped from Oporto.

12. Wicken Lode was mainly used to ship out turf to Cambridge. The drainage windmill on Wicken Sedge Fen was built as Norman's Mill on Adventure Fen in 1908 but was moved to Wicken Lode in about 1930. It is the only surviving Fen drainage windmill. Once 750 windmills pumped water on the three levels, of which 250 mills were on the Middle Level. Butterfly collectors purchased Wicken Sedge Fen between 1899-1911 and it was Britain's first nature reserve. Later on it became National Trust property.

13. Soham Lode was dug in about 1630 when the River Snail was diverted at Fordham from its original course to the River Lark at Prickwillow. The Lion Mill at the head of Soham Lode was built in 1811 and grain came in by Fen lighters and flour was shipped out. There was general trade up the Lode until the railway reached Soham in 1879 and trade had finished by about 1890.

14. Carr Dyke. A Roman canal for moving wheat from Reach to Lincoln.

15. Burwell. Means 'spring near the Fort'. There could have been a Roman fort here. In the Victorian period Burwell was a barge building centre and turf boats took the turf down to Upware to be loaded in barges for King's Lynn and Cambridge.

16. Burwell Lode. Because of the poor road system in the Fens, until after World War II, there was considerable lighter traffic from Burwell Lode. In 1898, barges shipped 8,600 tons of clunch from the quarry, bricks and fertilizer, out of Burwell Lode. Prentice Brothers fertilizer factory on Burwell Lode had its own barges and tugs taking fertilizer out to farms on the Fen, where the roads were very poor, until after World War II. In 1937 Vic Jackson's steam tug and gang of Fen lighters took about 2000 tons of fertilizer from Prentice Bros. on Burwell Lode to the farms.

17. In the 1860s the Upware public house 'Five Miles from Anywhere. No Hurry?' was renowned for 'prize fights' between bargemen. Under-graduates also came down to this then remote spot to get away from the authority of Cambridge University, and formed the 'Republic of Upware'. This hard drinking fellowship was presided over by the 'King of Upware' Richard Ramsay Fielder. The Upware ferry ran until 1950.

18. In 1915 river walls on the Little Ouse broke and some 40,000 acres were flooded. Because the nation's main energy was taken in fighting World War I the repairs were very slow. The water started off by being seven feet deep and two years later they had still only pumped it down to three feet. It took several years of hand-labour to repair the riverbanks. Barges took sugar beet from Lakenheath Lode to the Wissington Factory. In the 1947 floods the water first went over the walls where the farm sugar beet traffic had worn them down.

19. Dimmocks Cote. There was a ferry here until the road bridge was built in about 1931. A new road was constructed across Stretham Mere to a bridge over the Old West River (Great Ouse) that replaced a ford in about 1920.

20. Holywell. The holy well is near the church and it is claimed that the 'Ferryboat' Inn dates from about 980. The chain ferry ran until about 1949. There was a chain ferry at the 'Pike and Eel' Inn, Needingworth until about 1920 and a punt ferry operated until about 1948.

21. Castle Hythe was a medieval quay at the head of the river through Cawdle Fen. The railway stations at Ely, Littleport and Benwick all had quays so that coal could be shot straight into barges and taken out to the Fen villages.

22. Island of Babylon. Boat building at Ely from the end of the sixteenth century. Appleyard family moved their boat building yard across to the east bank of the Ely Ouse. Barges brought timber to a wharf below the 'Cutter' until about 1935 and in 2000 flats were being built here. In 1971 the Maltings were converted to a public hall and in 2000 the Maltings Granary below the footbridge was converted for craft shops.

23. For three hundred years, Kimmeridge clay, or 'gault' was taken by lighters out of Roswell pits to repair the riverbanks. Men loading the barges by hand were called 'gaulters' while men putting the clay on the river walls were called 'bankers'. Pits now used by Ely Sailing Club.

24. At the end of World War II the Oxford and Cambridge University Boat Races as rowed over a course between Littleport Bridge and Queen Adelaide.

25. Brandon. 9-10th Century Anglo-Saxon settlement with a church on an 'island' near the Little Ouse. In the medieval period the village moved up on to the higher ground possibly because water levels rose or it was simply an unhealthy site. The Thetford engineers Burrells built steel lighters and launched them sideways into the Little Ouse. They are also believed to have built the steam barge *Nancy*.

26. Hundred Foot Washes. In the seventeenth century the 4th Duke of Bedford, whose family had acquired the former great abbey estates of Whittlesey and Thorney, promoted the drainage of the Fens. The Dutch engineer Cornelius Vermuyden was hired to organize the draining of the Fens and he had the Bedford River dug in 1630 to speed up the Great Ouse course to The Wash. To improve on this the New Bedford River was dug in 1650. The area between the two Bedford Rivers is called the Hundred Foot Washes. In periods of heavy rain the Washes flood and this prevents flooding in other parts of this watercourse. In 1964 the Washes were leased to the RSPB, Wildfowl Trust and Cambridge Naturalist Trust.

27. Prickwillow Drainage Engine Museum. Prickwillow pumping station was opened in 1831, enlarged in 1880 and then diesel engines were installed in 1923. In 1958 there was

a new electric pumping station. Bridge restored 1900, new Low Bridge in 1962.

28.Isleham Lock was built and the new cut above it straightened out the Lark after the canalization of the River Lark to Bury St Edmunds started in 1635. This left an island of water meadows that were turned into Isleham Marina in 1988. In the nineteenth century Isleham Fen turf diggers used to take some of their turf to Cambridge. One man had his own small barge and pulled it by hand the 30 miles to Cambridge. He managed to do this twice a week, including at one point, unloading the barge, hauling it across a road and reloading it again. The Isleham Fen carrier E. W. Diver had a horse and gang of wooden lighters, but he later bought the tug *Bury* for the winter sugar beet work.

29.There used to be a ford and a ferry at Judes Ferry until the bridge was built in about 1895. The ford, until it was dredged away, continued to be used by the West Row Baptist Chapel for total immersion baptism.

30.Stretham Engine is the only preserved steam pump engine in the Black Fen. Built in 1831 it replaced four windmill pumps. The first steam pump in the Fens was at Sutton St Edmunds in 1817 and a larger pump was fitted at Deeping Fen. The Stretham engine, was in use until in 1940.

31.Hilgay earth works. Medieval manorial fish ponds off the River Wissey. In the 1947 Floods Hilgay Fen was under 15ft (4.5metres) of water. The floodwater knocked down houses at Southery. The Floods resulted from very heavy rainfall in 1946 followed by 12 inches (30 centimeters) of heavy snow in the first three months of 1947. When the snow thawed there was more heavy rain, but the ground was still frozen so it could not soak in. With a sudden rise in the river levels ice floes blocked the rivers and water poured over the banks.

32. About 1830 William Springfield owned the lime kilns at Stoke Ferry and had barges bringing up coal and lime trade seems to have finished by the time the railway arrived in 1882. However J Coston of Hilgay revived the trade in the 1890s with the steam barge *Wissey*. Vic Jackson took corn away from Stoke Ferry in the 1930s. Most of the sugar beet grown along the Wissey went by rail to the factory, so the barges loading at Stoke Ferry took the beet to Ely.

33. The opening of the sugar beet factory at Wissington in 1925 bought commercial traffic back to the Fen waterways. The Wissington factory had three tugs, *Wissington*, *Littleport* and *Hilgay* and 24 steel barges bringing coal up from Lynn in the summer and sugar beet in from the farms in the winter. A bomb sank the *Littleport* at King's Lynn in 1943 and after this it was decided to end the water transport section to Wissington and run the tugs and barges from Ely.

34. Barges went up to Oxborough Hythe until at least 1858. There was also a ferry here. There were boathouses further up steam at Northwold.

35. After the serious floods of 1936, 1937 and 1947 The Relief Cut-Off Channel was dug in three sections between 1954-64. This new twenty-eight mile channel with its thirty-five new bridges was cut through chalk and took the extra flood water that the Hundred Foot Washes could not store. The work to widen and deepen the Ely Ouse for nineteen miles was completed in 1961.

36. Denver Sluice. Key point in the drainage of the Fens. First closed in 1651 in spite of much protest from Cambridge and other inland towns. This prevented tidal water and sea going ships from going inland. After this goods for the inland towns were unloaded at King's Lynn and taken inland by lighter. In 1717 a very high tide smashed down Denver Sluice and it was not rebuilt until 1749. Since 1971 much of the water from the Ouse has been pumped from the Ely Ouse across country to reservoirs in Essex.

37. King's Lynn sugar beet factory originally used water transport. It had the steam tug *Jeanie Hope* and two large barges *Expectant* that loaded 140 tons and the *Blue* 200 tons that used to bring coal from the Alexandra Dock, King's Lynn. The traffic stopped in 1947 when the tug was sold to Vic Jackson.

38. Mullicourt Aqueduct, Outwell was built in 1848 to allow the Well Creek to pass over the Middle Level Main Drain.

This was part of a major scheme between 1844-48 when the Sixteen-Foot Drain was extended ten miles to the north. Nordelph 'Chequers' dates from around 1780. Public staithe at Nordelph constructed by Well Creek Trust.

39. Well Creek ceased to be tidal in 1556 when the Dean of Ely and Sir Edmund Beaupe built the Salter's Lode sluice. Most of the sugar beet grown on the farms around the Middle Level Navigations went by barge to the Wissington factory until the end of 1958. The tugs had great problems with the tides when entering Salters Lode and the New Bedford River. Loaded barges could only be taken through Salters Lode lock one at a time, and a second tug had to be on hand to tow the barges up to Denver Sluice.

40. Roman farms at Eastrea and Coates, near March and in the Ramsey area. In medieval times Ramsey Abbey was one of the large monastic landowners who began the first serious drainage of the Fens.

41. Morton Leam was a twelve-mile channel, cut by Bishop Morton of Ely in 1487 to improve drainage in the Black Fen. Morton Leam straightened the Nene between Stanground and Guyhirn. Stanground was a centre for Fen barges. Both A.V.Jackson (Peterborough) Ltd and W.Lee had boat yards here and these two became Stanground Boatyard Ltd.

42. In the medieval period the monks of Thorney Abbey developed Woodston as the port for their market at Yaxley. After the railway arrived at Peterborough, Woodston wharf went out of use. Some Fen lighter hulks remain near the bridge on Orton Mere, but they are only exposed when the water is very low.

43. Nene Washes created in 1728 when the Nene and Morton's Leam were straightened. The old course of the Nene went from Peterborough across to Ramsey and March and through Well Creek to join up with the Great Ouse.

44. Wisbech Canal, which linked the Well Creek to Wisbech, was opened in 1795. Allowed to silt up after the Wisbech & Upwell Tramway was opened in 1883. This closed in about 1923. The Wisbech Canal has since been filled in and the end is under a bungalow garden. The western part of Well Creek is the old course of the River Nene where it ran through to join up with the Great Ouse. Most of the rivers and drains in the Fens have been rerouted over the centuries. The Well Creek fell into disrepair, but was reopened for navigation in 1975.

45. Thorney River closed to navigation in 1930 when the 'Dog in a Doublet' Lock was enlarged. The tide had flowed up Woodston Staunch beyond Peterborough and after the new lock was built this was then blown up.

46. There was a railway yard and a dock for Fen lighters at March. March had two 'drops' where sugar beet were loaded for Wissington, and other drops at Floods Ferry, Benwick and Ramsey.

47. The East Lighthouse is at the River Nene outfall into the Wash. The two 'light houses' at the outfall were actually built as worker's cottages, after a new cut was dug in 1830. The old river course was dammed and 900 men with 250 horses worked to dig the seven mile Nene Outfall Cut between Wisbech and the Wash. Sir Peter Scott, the wild life artist, leased the East Lighthouse from 1933-39.

48. Whittlesey Mere was the largest natural lake in southern England. In the 1770s the Earl of Sandwich kept his yacht *Whittlesey* on the Mere and Regattas were held here later. Whittlesey Mere was drained in 1851 because the Middle Level drainage system had been improved. As the Mere dried out, stones, a silver incense boat and silver chandelier belonging to Ramsey Abbey were found. No doubt they had been in craft that had sunk on the way to Ramsey Abbey. Ramsey Mere and the other meres had been drained earlier.

49. Vic Jackson's last gang of barges was sold to the Nene Barge & Lighter Company in 1945 after they had been used to ship stone out for river wall maintenance. Later the barges were sunk in their Ship End Quarry.

50. Around 1900 H. J. Groom ran a ferry at Dentford. From his boathouse he also ran a boat building and hire business.

51. Wellingborough earth works are medieval fishponds.

52. In the 1947 flood the banks 'blew' at Crowland on the

River Welland and flooded 20,000 acres to form a lake of 20 square miles.

53. There was barge traffic to Stamford until 1863 and the trade to Spalding petered out in about 1935. About 1912 there was a trial freight up to Spalding with the 103ft coastal steam ship *Mistley*. She was unable to get up to the quay so they had to discharge her in the middle of the river and this held up all the river traffic for several days.

54. River Glen was made navigable by an act of 1781 and there was barge traffic until 1857.

55. Early Pilgrim Fathers sailed for America from Scotia Creek in 1607, but were arrested and brought back. Boston Haven is the mouth of the River Witham that was straightened between 1828-9. Boston Dock dug in 1882.

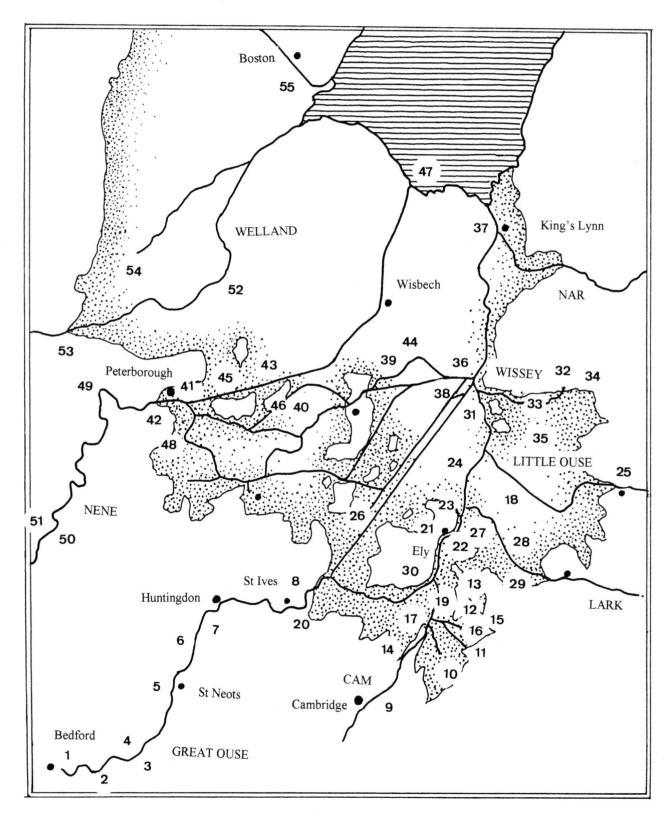

Chapter Three

THE RIVER NENE AND DOWN TO THE MIDDLE LEVEL.

122. The narrow boat *Enigma* approaching Lock 17 on the Northampton Arm of the Grand Union Canal. In the background is the transit shed built in about 1925. The *Enigma* was going to the island, at Northampton, for the November the fifth fireworks event in 1999.

123. The 70ft *Grange,* a narrow boat built in 1912, going through Lock 17 on the Northampton Arm of the Grand Union Canal in 1999. This lovely little canal is the only link between the inland waterways system of England and the Rivers Nene and Great Ouse, but the locks only have a width of 7ft so they are not accessible to many modern power craft.

124. Flooding after the heavy rain at Easter 1998 at Billing Aquadrome. The 250acre Aquadrome site had been flooded to create five lakes for recreation after being gravel pits.

125. Narrow boats at the Weetabix Mills, Wellingborough in 1966. The British Waterways' narrow boats brought around 5,000 tons of imported wheat a year from Brentford Dock up the Grand Union Canal. This ended in 1969 when grain imports were moved from London docks down to the Grain Terminus at Tilbury. The Wellingborough Mill closed in 1999.

126. Woodford Mill on the River Nene in 1902. Work on constructing locks to turn the River Nene into the navigation for barge traffic started in 1724 and was completed in 1761. There was limited traffic before this with small 1-3 ton boats that were unloaded and then dragged over land each time there was an obstacle.

127. The official opening of Oundle Marina in 1964. The three cruisers were part of the Newington's Enterprize Hire Fleet, which was operated here from 1963-88. The hire fleet was *Jaunty, Jolly, Jovial, Merry* and *Gay* and all these names ended in *Enterprise*.
This ballast pit was dug during World War II to find material to make the runways for the aerodromes the USAF used. After the war J. T. 'Jack' Newington purchased the flooded pit and dug a channel through to the River Nene so that he and his RAF friends could keep their boats there. The site of Oundle Marine Chandery is on the right while the ballast machine is in the pit, which is now the Country Park across the Barnwell Road.

128. Jack Newington at the opening of Oundle Marina by Roger Pilkington in 1964. As Oundle Marina grew Jack Newington started a hire fleet and began building cabin cruisers. This became a separate business, run beside Oundle Marina, making the Fairline cruisers. Started by Jack Newington and later run by his son Sam Newington, Fairline employed 680 people in 1998. They worked on three sites and had become the largest small boat-manufacturing firm in Britain.

129. Alwalton Lynch in about 1908. This is the second lock above Peterborough of the thirty-seven locks in sixty miles of the River Nene.

The Nene is well known for its flash floods, and different pronunciation of its name. Below Peterborough it is usually the 'Neen', but further up in Northampton it is usually called the 'Nen'.

130. The river front at Peterborough in 1906 seen from Wood Fair Meadow. In the 1840s the boat builder Ellington, had a yard at a site in the centre of the picture. Later Hemment's had a boatyard in a wooden barn on the river frontage and this was replaced by a slip in the centre. After Hemment's, the Engineers Peak had the buildings. The area was redeveloped in the 1980s and only the Custom's House on the extreme right has survived.

131. A Fen barge loading stone at Peterborough Town Bridge about 1907. The 'sprit' (steering pole) can be seen on the bow. The original London Road Town Bridge was wooden, but there was a Victorian iron bridge that was replaced in 1928. Bridge Street was flooded in 1848 and 1875. In the 1848 flood a boat was rowed up Bridge Street as far as the 'Golden Lion' and the stalls at Peterborough Bridge Fair were swept away.

Peterborough Bridge

132. Peterborough Town Bridge in about 1900.

133. The Peterborough Warship being towed up to Peterborough by Vic Jackson in 1947. In about 1942 the Sea Scouts took over the Custom's House, which had been built in about 1770. After World War II the Admiralty gave the Peterborough Sea Scouts the *MTB 777* which was a Fairmile D, built at Bangor in 1944. The firm Gabriel, Wade and English had timber brought in from Wisbech to the wharf on the right.

134. The *Peterborough Trader,* a coaster built in Holland in 1915, being loaded with 65,000 bricks at Peterborough Quay in 1938 just below the Custom's House. The 'Dog in a Doublet' lock was enlarged and the river dredged deeper and in 1938 Peterborough was officially opened as an inland port. The first ship to arrive was Harker's 119ft tanker *Constance* H. The Stanground barge owner Vic Jackson was very keen to promote Peterborough as a port and he purchased the 250ton *Peterborough Trader,* and 225ton, *Peterborough Merchant.* These two coasters used to take bricks to Hull and return with cattle food, a trade that lasted until World War II.

Astern of the *Peterborough Trader* is Vic Jackson's gang of Fen barges. The main trade for them was to bring timber from the ships at Wisbech up to Peterborough. Jackson's barges were towed up by horse until the steam tug was purchased in 1938.

135. Vic Jackson at the tiller of his new 36ft pleasure-launch *Queen of the Nene.* This launch did trips in the 1950s, mainly evening runs, with up to fifty-five passengers. The river frontage was developed in about 1972 as a mooring for pleasure boats and given the name Peterborough Key.

Vic Jackson, who came from March, married Ivy Lee, member of the barge family, and started off as a carrier with the barges. Once in the 1930s, it took him seven weeks to go from Wisbech to Northampton with a gang of barges, because of a drought, but he did the next trip in four days.

Jackson, known as 'The Admiral', was very enterprising and was always thinking up new ideas to earn a living from the water. In the 1930s he was a barge and ship owner based at 77 North Street, Stanground. He then bought 47-73 North Street and had a barge repair yard there, but after World War II the Admiralty took over his coasters and in 1945 he sold his Fen barges to the Nene Barge & Lighter Co. He then changed to yacht building

136. There was a Regatta in about 1960, on the Peterborough Embankment. Mr Cobin and Vic Jackson were judging the smartest boat competition. The barge in the background is discharging at the Flour Rolling Mill.

137. The auxiliary Thames sailing barge *Thyra* waiting to discharge wheat from Hull at the Flour Rolling Mill, at Peterborough in 1961. The Mill was built with an archway underneath it so that Fen barges could go in to discharge under cover.

As well as the *Thyra* the London & Rochester Trading Co. sent their auxiliary barges *Pudge*, *Varuna* and *Alan* to Peterborough. They usually brought imported grain from Hull docks and sometimes from the London docks. In spite of the difficulties of getting up the Nene *Thyra* earned her crew of two good wages, because she loaded English wheat from Peterborough to the Co-op Mills at Hull, and returned with imported wheat. Barge traffic to Peterborough ended in about 1971.

138. The Thames barges *Veravia* and *Thyra* at the Peterborough Flour Rolling Mill in 1957. Tony Winter, mate of the *Thyra,* is sitting on *Veravia's* rail, and the skipper of this barge was Fred 'Nelson' Wilson. The owner Nick Hardinge sailed as mate.

On the opposite side of the river are the motor hire boats that were owned by Vic Jackson and operated by Peter and Sheila Conning. Hire boats owned by Ted Hammond operated from the same inlet. The Council placed restrictions on the people who hired out boats and this made them give up in about 1959.

139. Vic Jackson, with his new boat lift, at his Stanground Yard in about 1950. Vic Jackson had switched from commercial shipping to boat building. He bought ship's lifeboats, off ships being broken up on the Clyde, and converted them to fishing boats. He also converted ex- Admiralty craft into pleasure boats.

140. Peter Conning standing in one of the boats he built at Vic Jackson's Stanground Yard in North Street in the 1950s. This boat was known on the yard as 'The Coffin'.

141. The barge *Veravia* in 'Dog in a Doublet' lock, in 1957 loaded with Canadian wheat for the Peterborough Mill. She was on a regular charter and once, during the summer, when coming up to this lock she grounded through lack of water and was held up for two days.

Above: 142. The auxiliary barge *Veravia*, with her gear lowered, going under the Guyhirn Bridge while on passage from Hull to Peterborough with 160 tons of Canadian wheat from Hull. The London and Rochester barges traded up here so regularly that the crews painted marks on the bridges and locks to give them a guide as to how high the tide was.

With the tide in the Nene flowing nine hours on the ebb (out), and only three hours on the flood (in), it took two daylight tides to get from Big Ann's buoy at the entrance up to Peterborough. The most difficult piece of navigation for barges on the Nene was crossing The Brink, an area just above Wisbech Bridge where there were a lot of stones on the riverbed. The *Thyra* came up to the old Wisbech Bridge on a tide and the Skipper Reg Martin was particularly good at judging when the tide was right to go under the low bridge and over The Brink.

It was more difficult coming down as they had to drop a kedge anchor over the stern and stop to wait for the tide to be high enough to get over The Brink, but under the bridge. Once after heavy rain the kedge failed to stop the *Thyra* and she banged over The Brink. This caused considerable damage to her wooden bottom.

Right: 143. This shows Ivy Jackson, in a punt in about 1938, on The Backwater at Stanground. She was about to ferry a fresh horse over the other side, to replace the tired horse in a gang of barges that was coming from Wisbech. Once on the island the horse would have been taken across the Nene on the 'Hos' (Horse) Ferry, near the Black Bridge, and from there the Jackson children rode the horse some seven miles down to the 'Dog in a Doublet'. The tired horse either rode back on a barge or was ridden back to the stables at Stanground.

144. Three gangs of A.V. Jackson's Fen barges at Wisbech in 1933. Leading the horse on the left is twenty-seven year old Vic Jackson. The two men from each gang lived in the cabin in the middle of the house lighter. This space had a bunk on either side and a coal burning stove in the middle and was very warm and snug in the winter. Vic Jackson was very fond of meat so he used to buy a sack full of meat from a butcher near the river. The vegetables they robbed out of the fields as they went past, also a chicken and duck, if they could get away with it. No wonder the bargemen were unpopular with country people. They had a stock pot boiling on the stove all the time and a kettle of very stewed tea.

145. A Fen 'house lighter' at the Outwell Sluice end of the Wisbech Canal in about 1908. This canal was opened in 1796 closed in 1922 and then filled in.

146. Dennis Barrett in 1985 with his three narrow boats he hired out from Upwell. Dennis had come from Kingston in 1981 to establish a hire boat business on Well Creek.

147. The timber ships at Wisbech in September 1861. In the early nineteenth century, ships could not get up to Wisbech and goods were put into barges at Sutton Bridge.

2105 Unloading Timber Boats, Wisbech.

148. Timber ships discharging at East Quay, Wisbech in about 1938. Timber was one of the most important freights delivered to Wisbech.

149. The wooden Danish built barque *Earl of Pembroke* visiting the East Quay, Wisbech in 1998 to 'heighten awareness of the port'. As ships have grown larger the smaller ports, which boomed in the 1970s, have lost trade. A marina for pleasure craft was opened at Wisbech at around this time.

150. The auxiliary sailing barge *Thyra* passing through Sutton Bridge bound from Hull with wheat, her last cargo up to Peterborough, in about 1967. Robert Stephenson built the first bridge across the Nene in 1850 and the swing bridge was built in 1897. After this there was an attempt to start a port here. In 1967 the bridge was being opened for seven ships a week, but in 2000 Malcolm Fairweather was opening the bridge for three ships a week.

151. Shell fish being unloaded from the smacks at the Mussel Stage, Skirbeck Quarter, Boston in 1928. Because of the fast tides in the Wash few fish came in so that the smacks working from Boston, Wisbech and King's Lynn concentrated on prawn, shrimp, mussel and cockle.

152. The Boston smack *Alice* in August 1921. The Boston smacks had to sail down the narrow 7-mile Boston Haven before they reached the open waters of the Wash. Because the Wash smacks worked in narrow channels they carried a powerful gaff cutter rig and had fine bows which fishermen said made them 'go to windward like a knife'.